Green Umbrella Coloring Book Volume 1

Fruity Faces

Joyce Mitchell

KIDS!!

Each 'Fruity Face' has a name! What a fun book! ENJOY!!!

Apple
Banana
Blackberry
Cantaloupe
Cherry
Coconut
Fig
Grapefruit
Grapes
Kiwi
Lemon
Mango
Orange
Papaya
Peach
Pear
Pineapple
Plum
Pomegranate
Strawberry
Watermelon

DREAM – CREATE – INSPIRE
DON'T FORGET YOUR 'DOODLE' PAGE

Also, Check out:
GREEN UMBRELLA Coloring Book for Kids and Adults: Volume 2:
ALPHABET (Black Background)

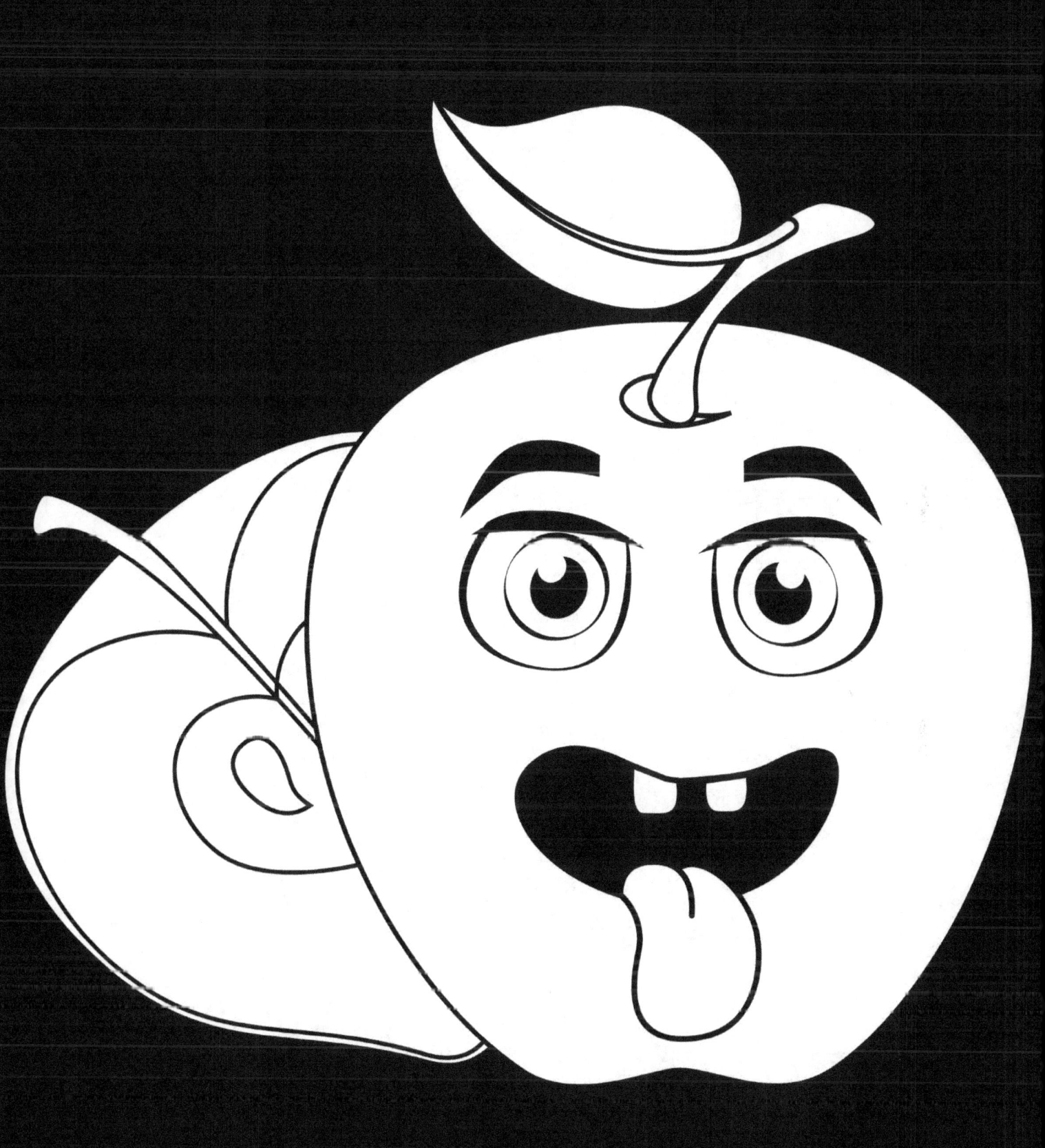

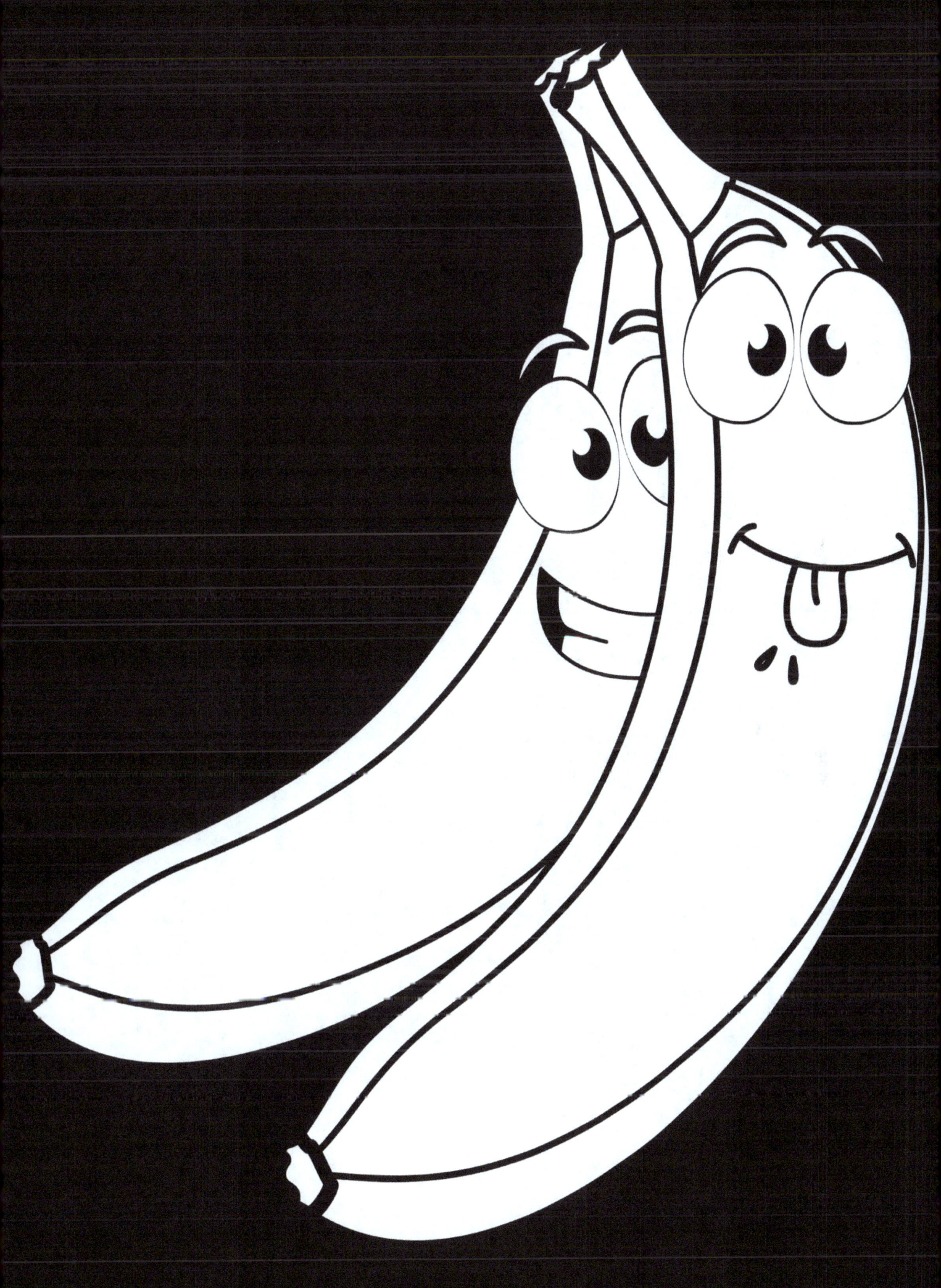

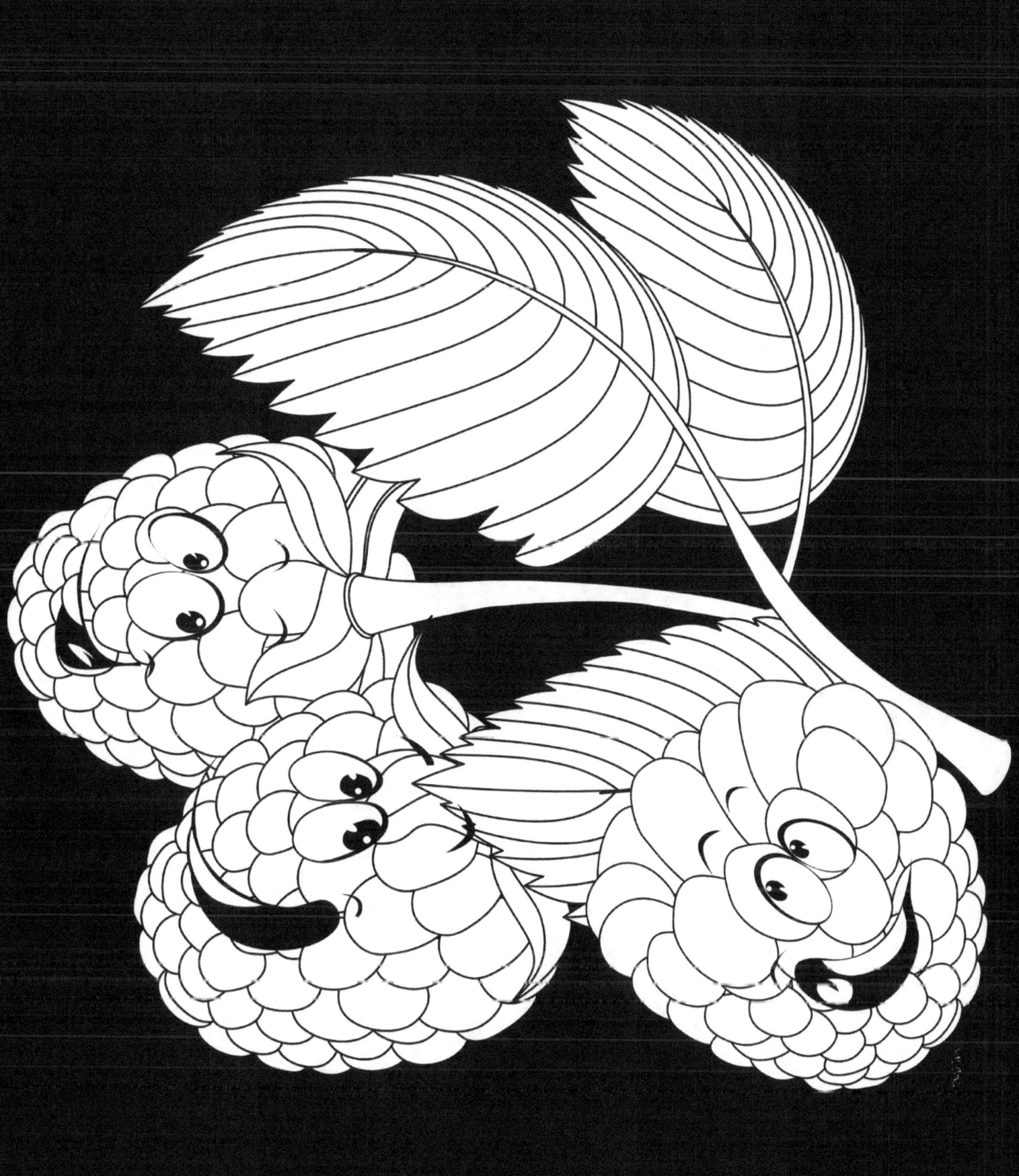

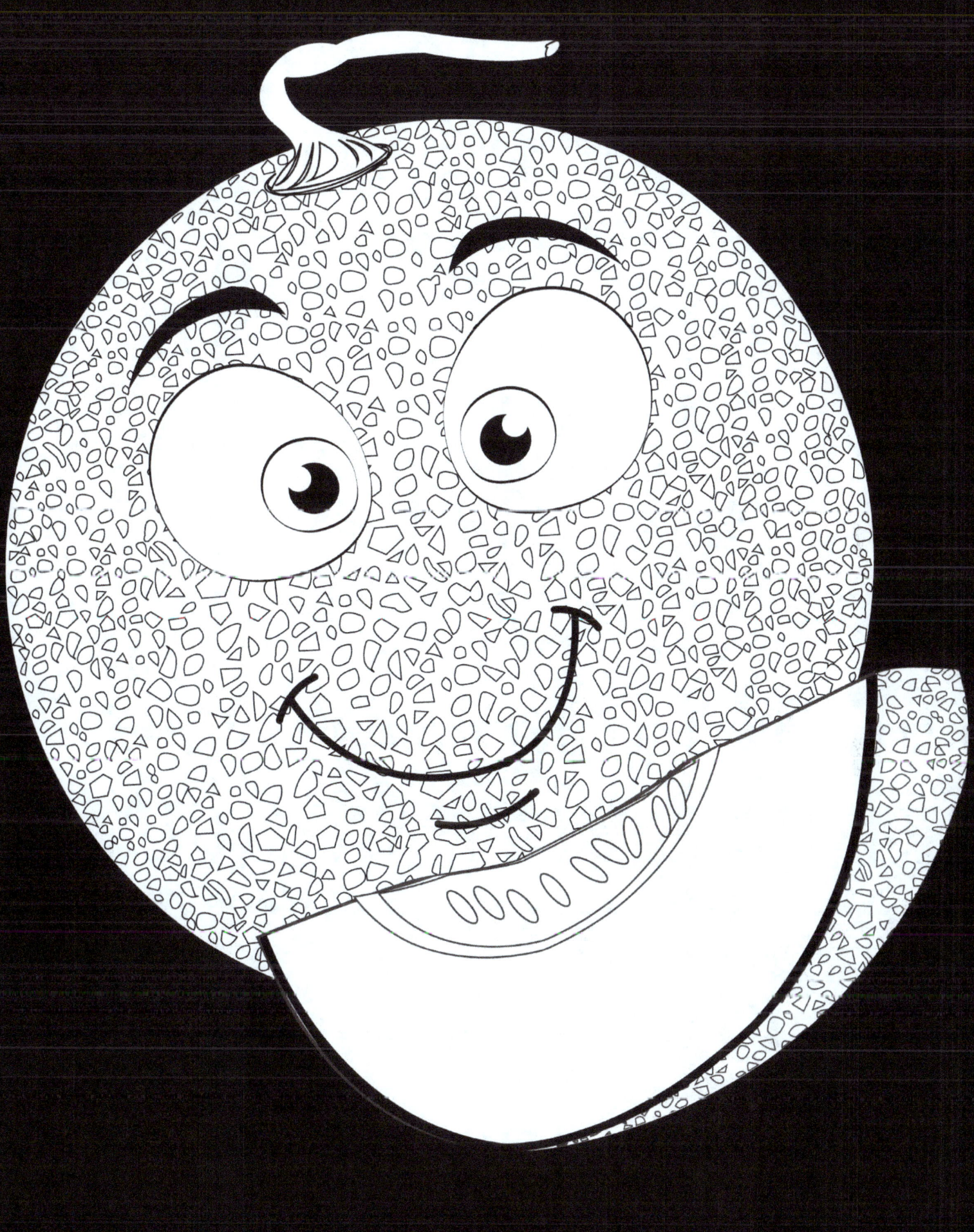

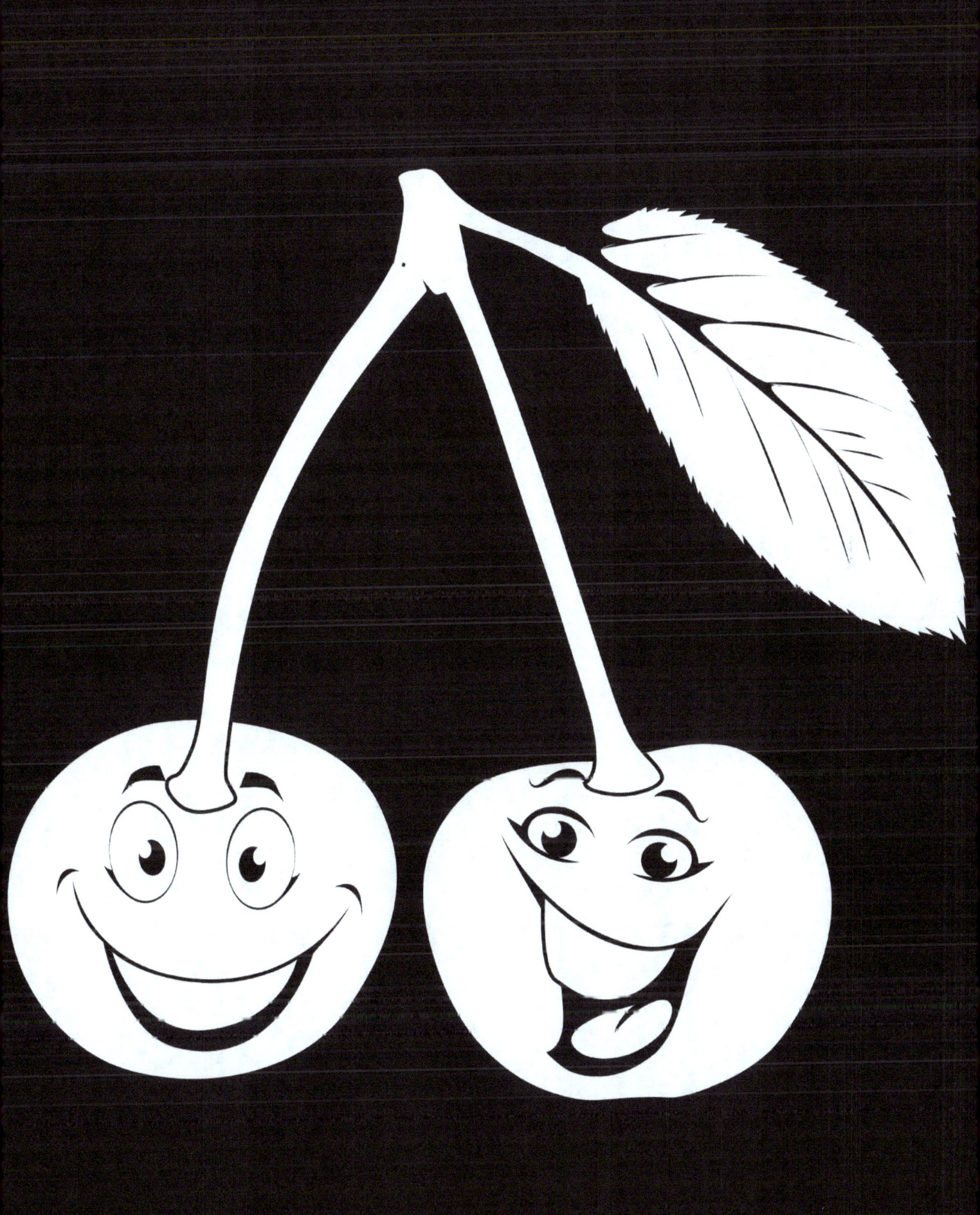

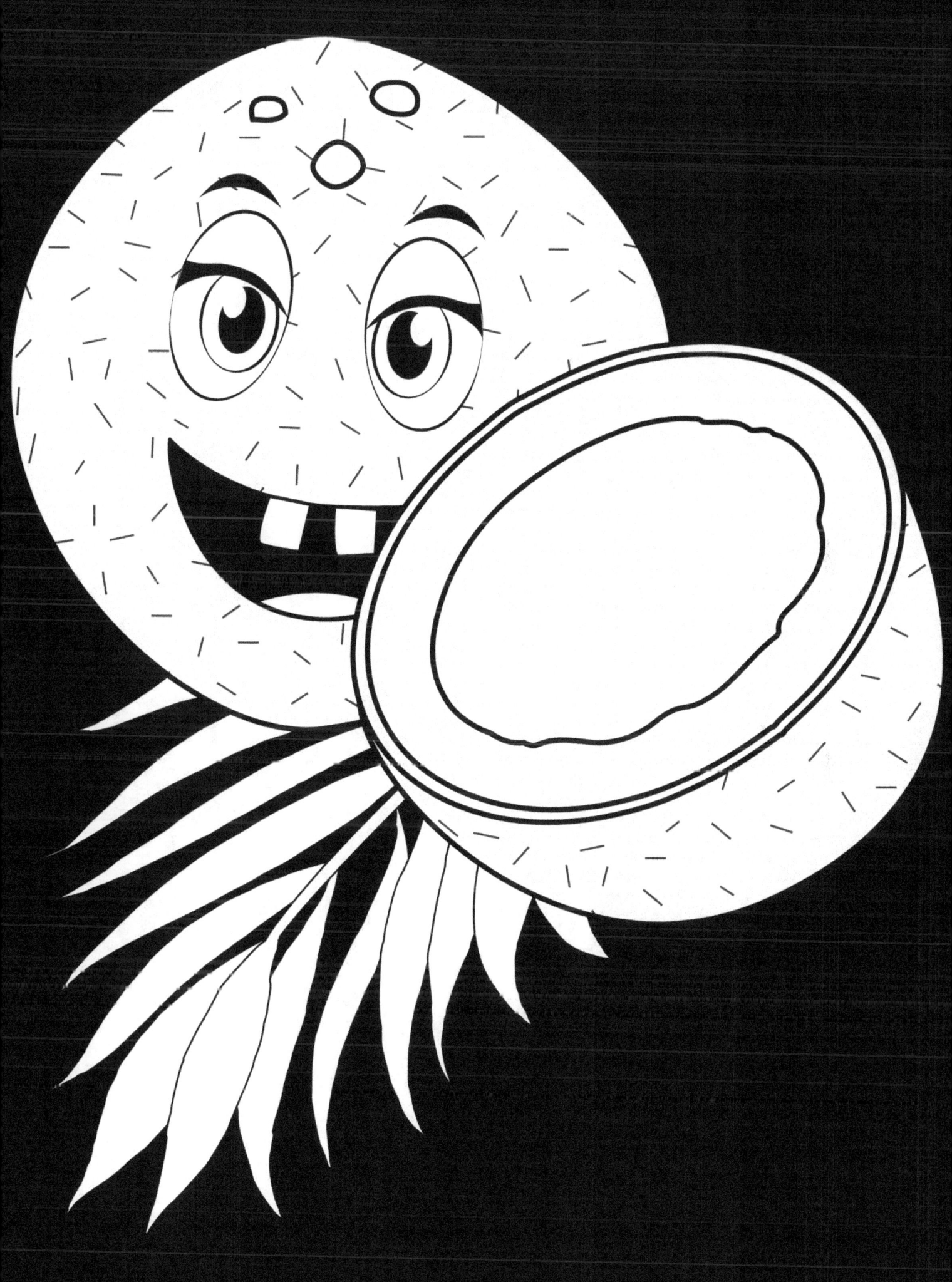

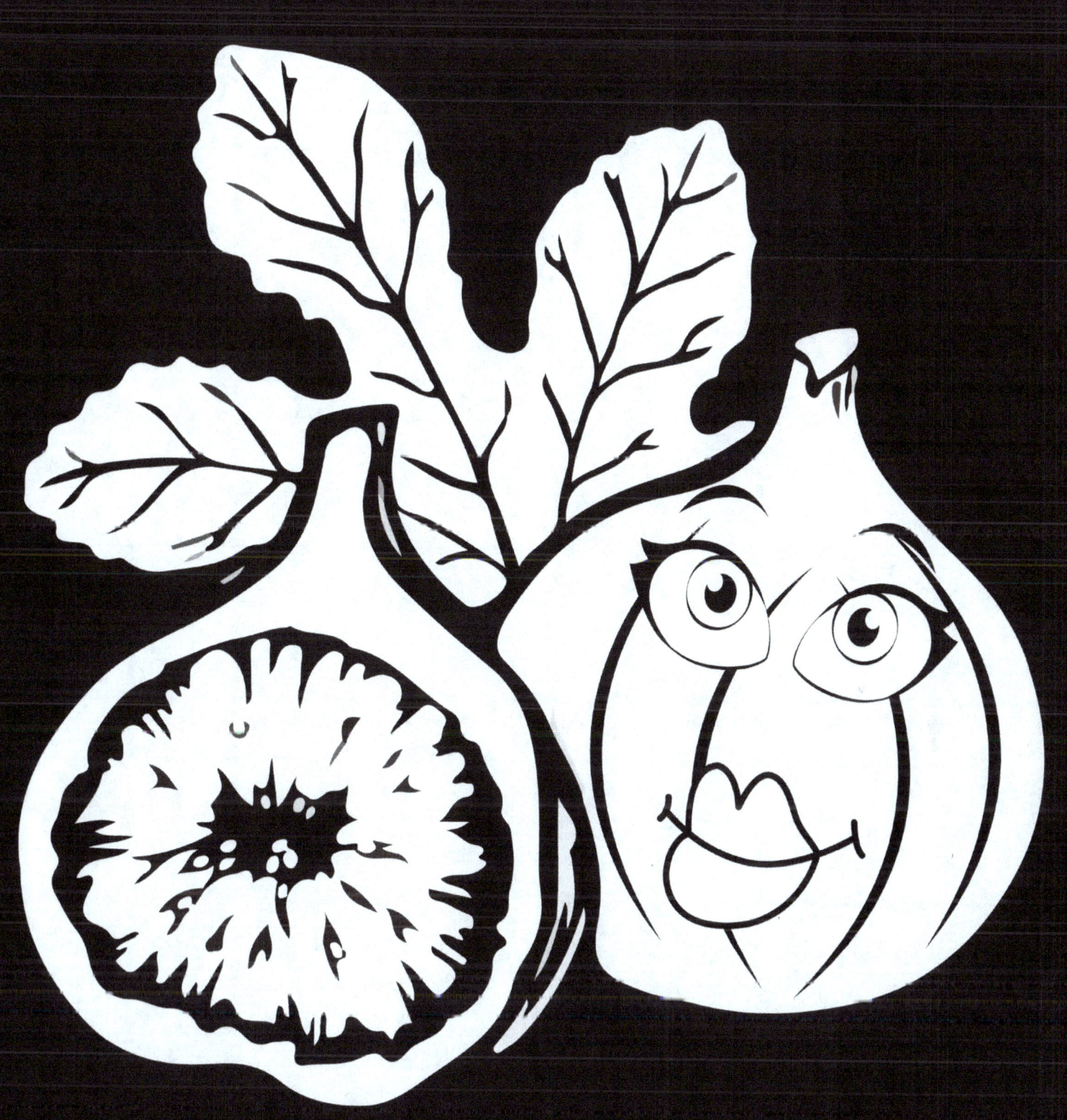

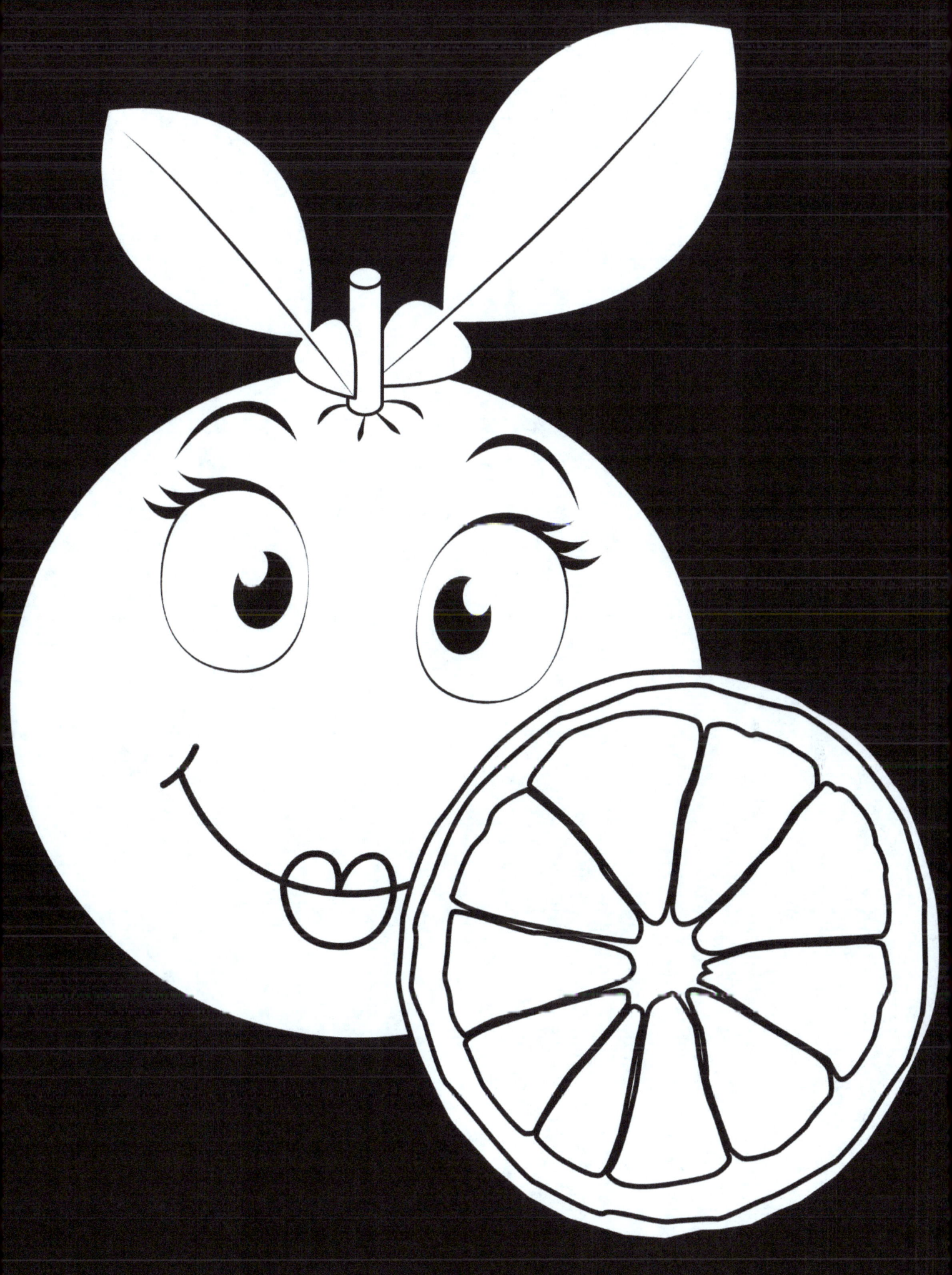

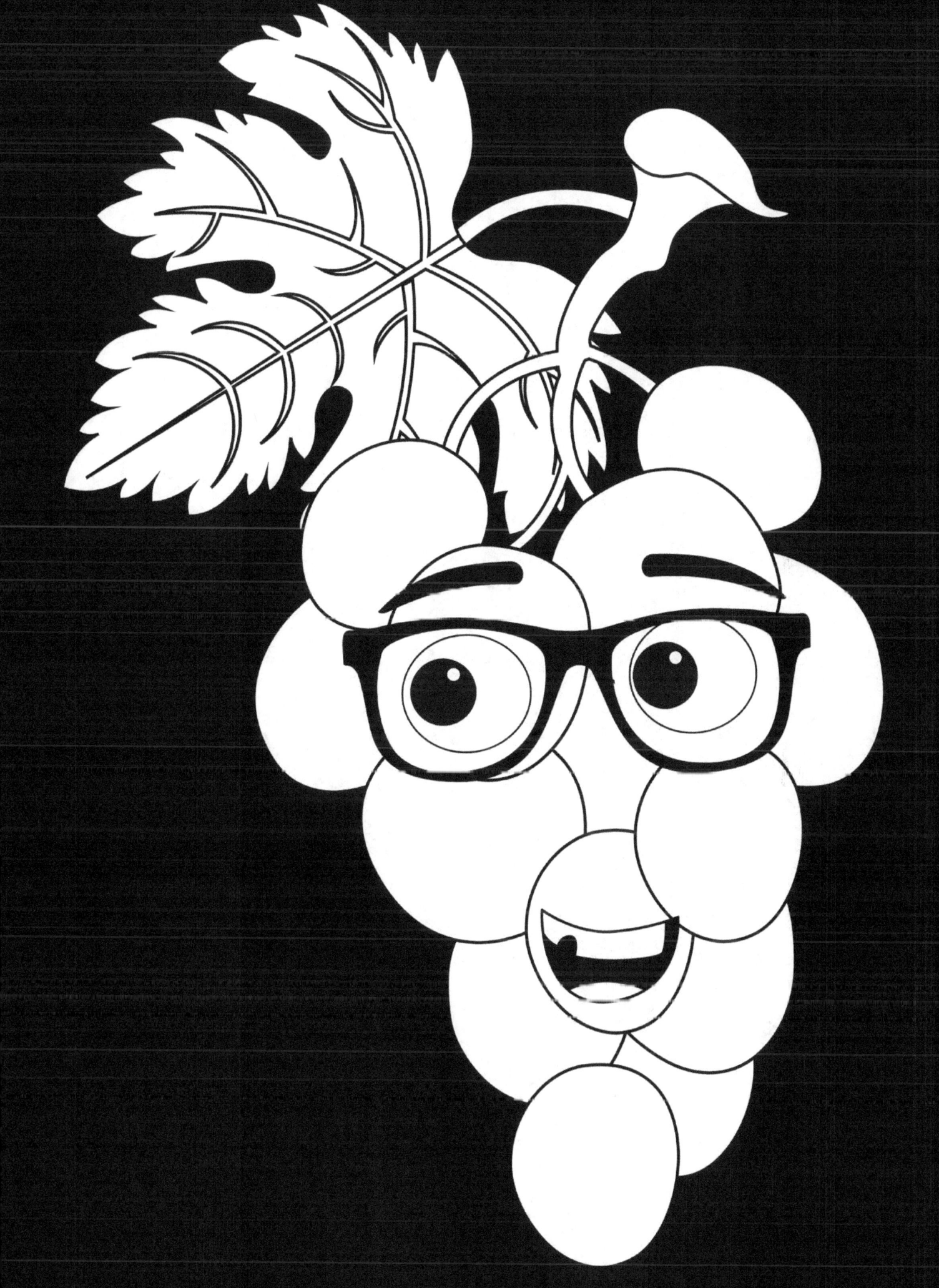

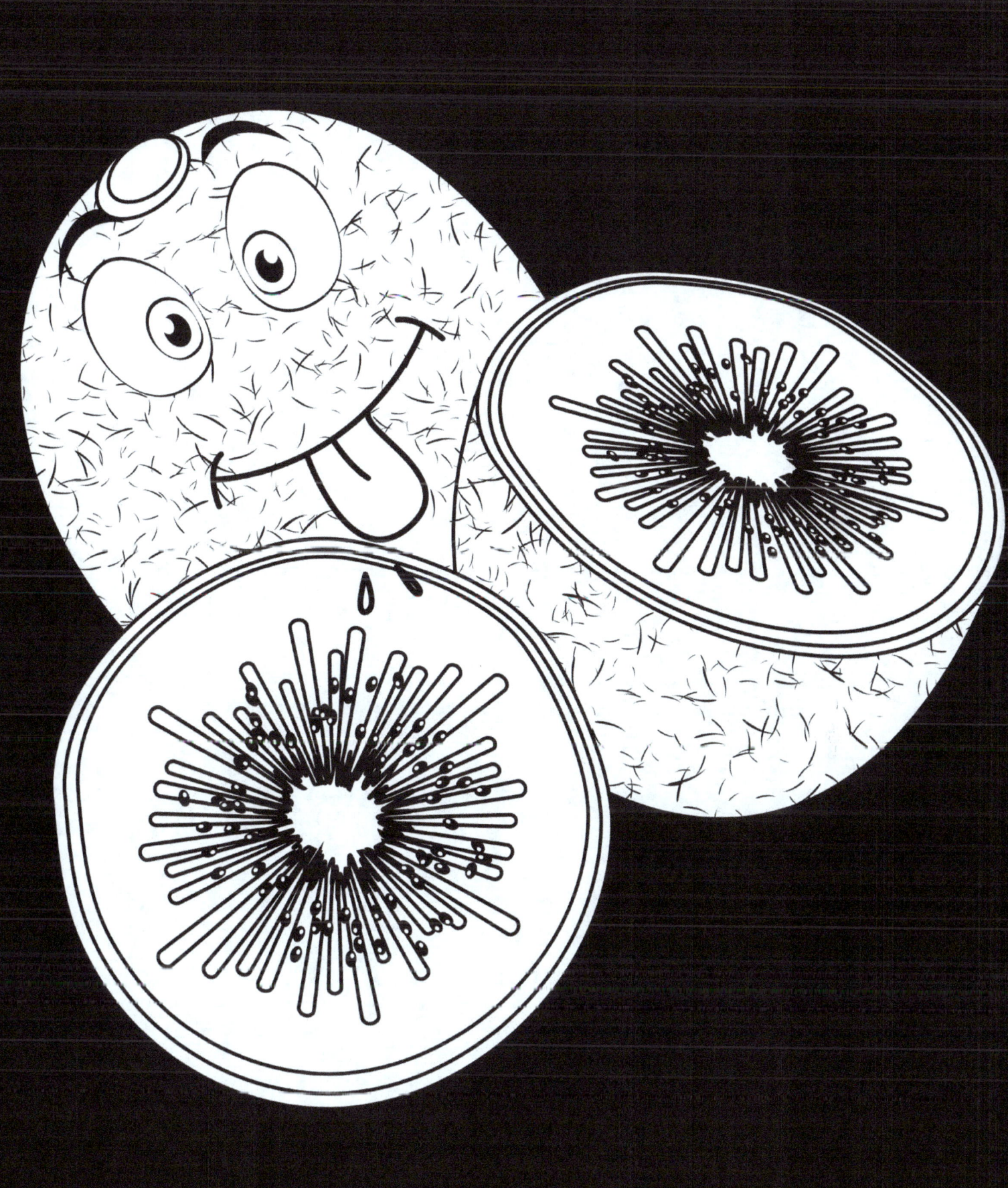

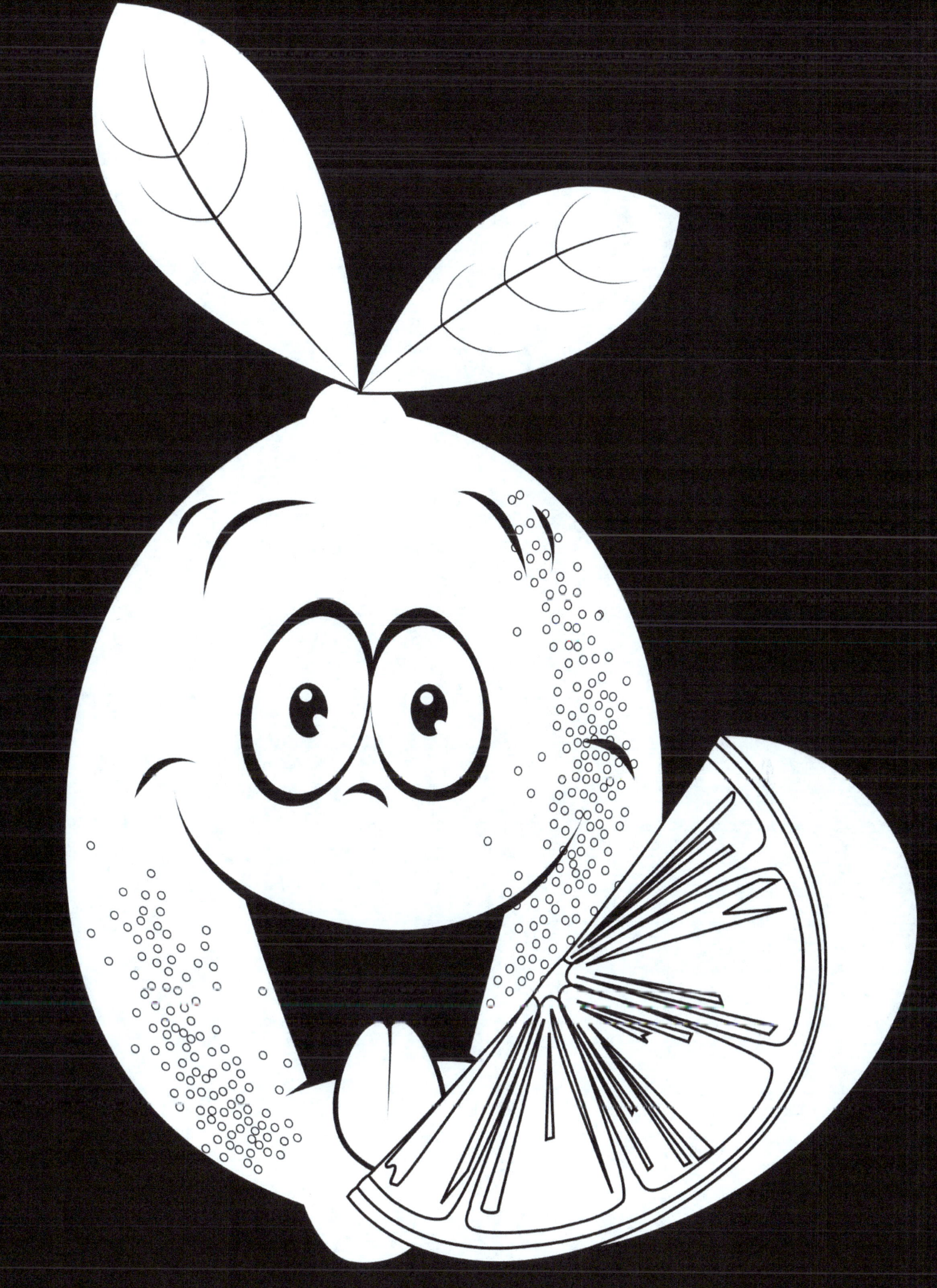

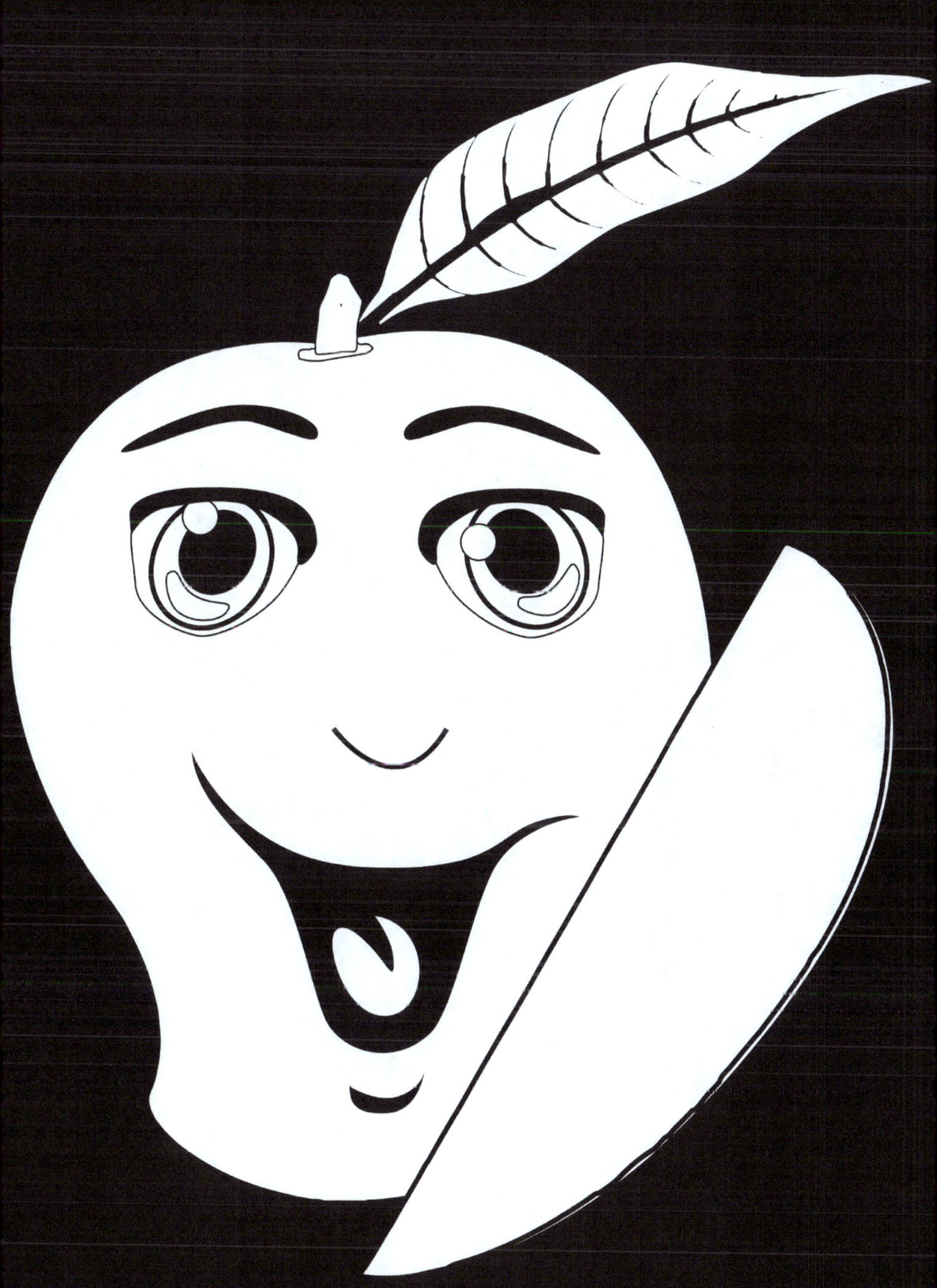

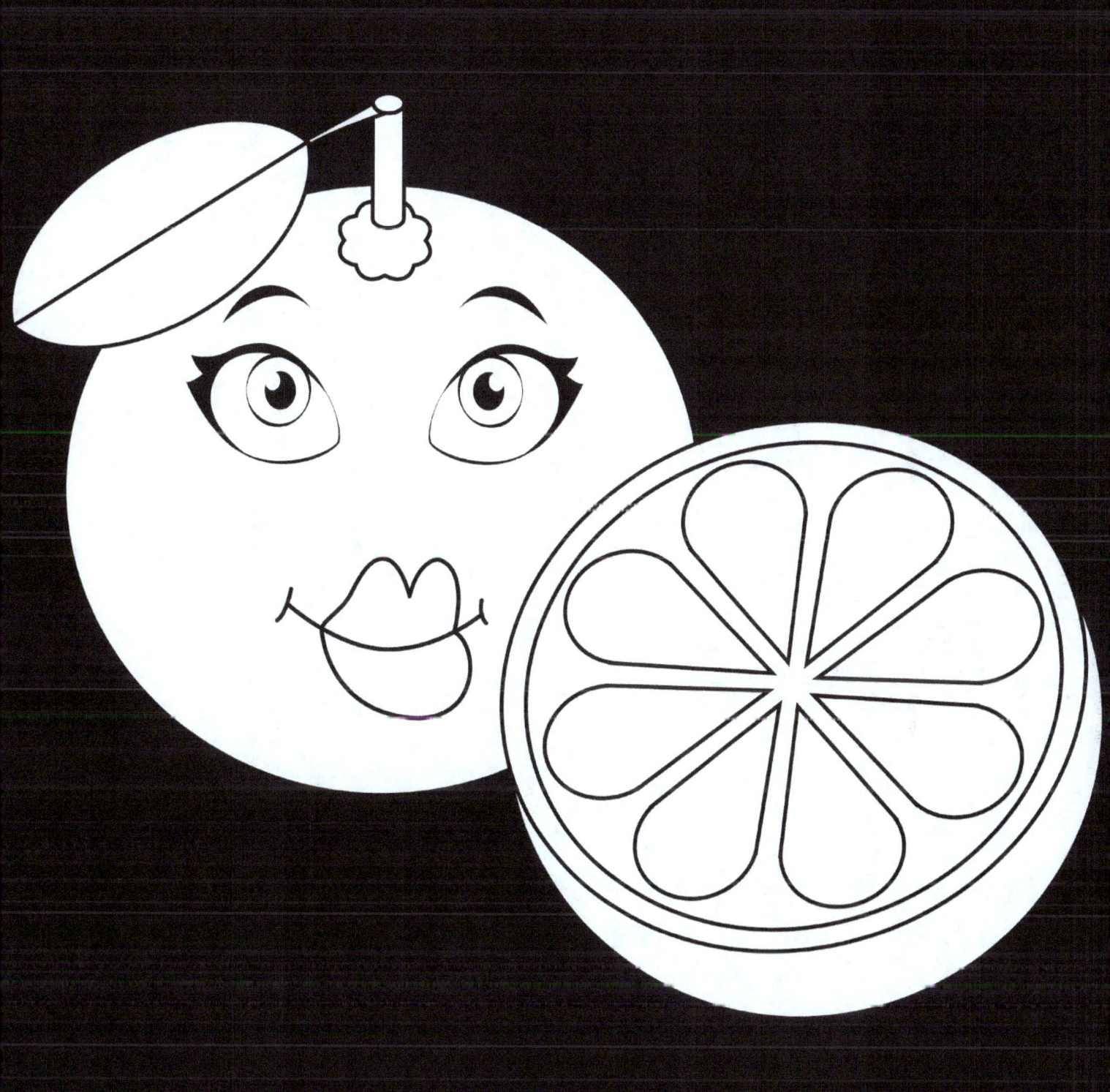

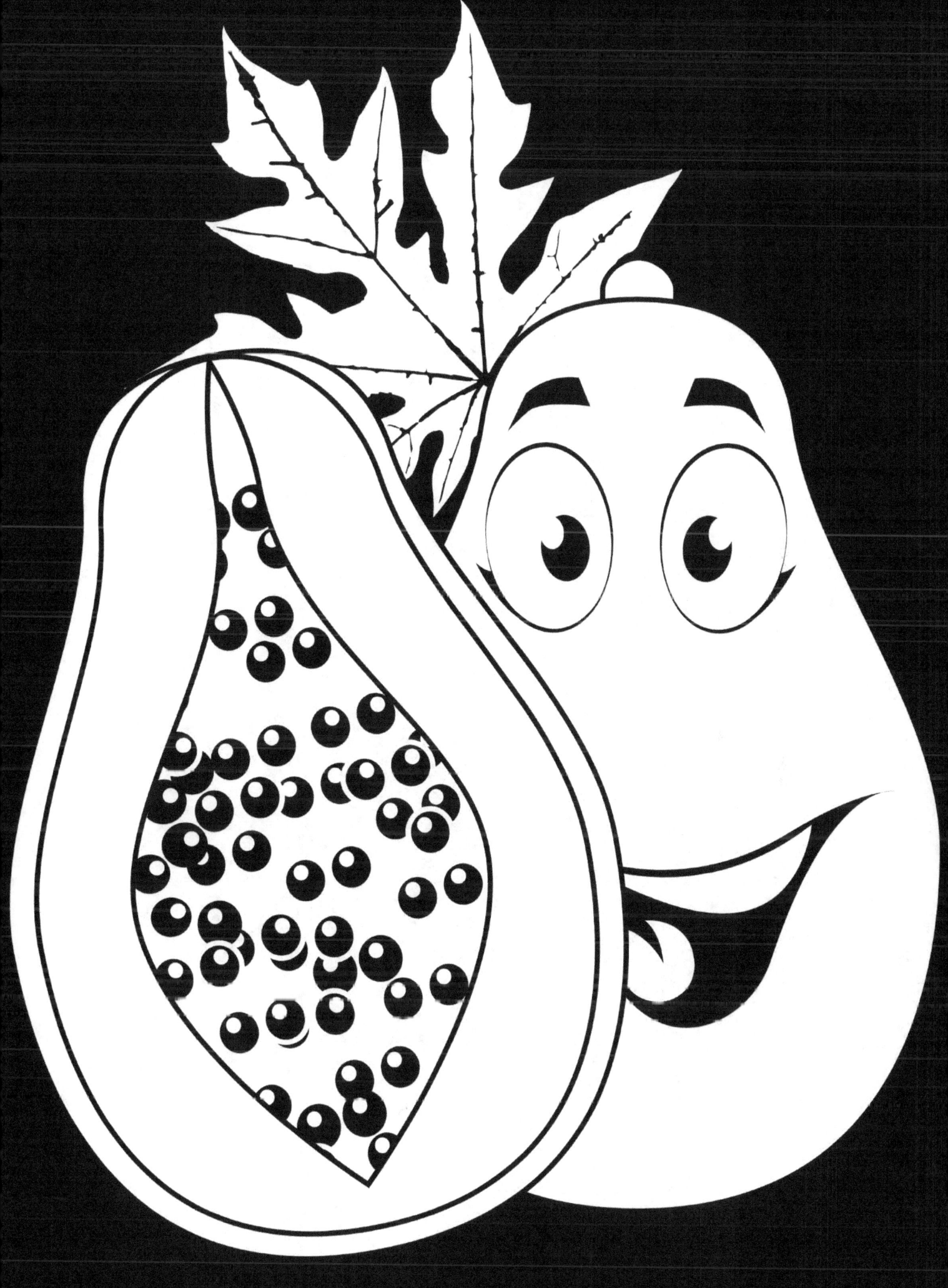

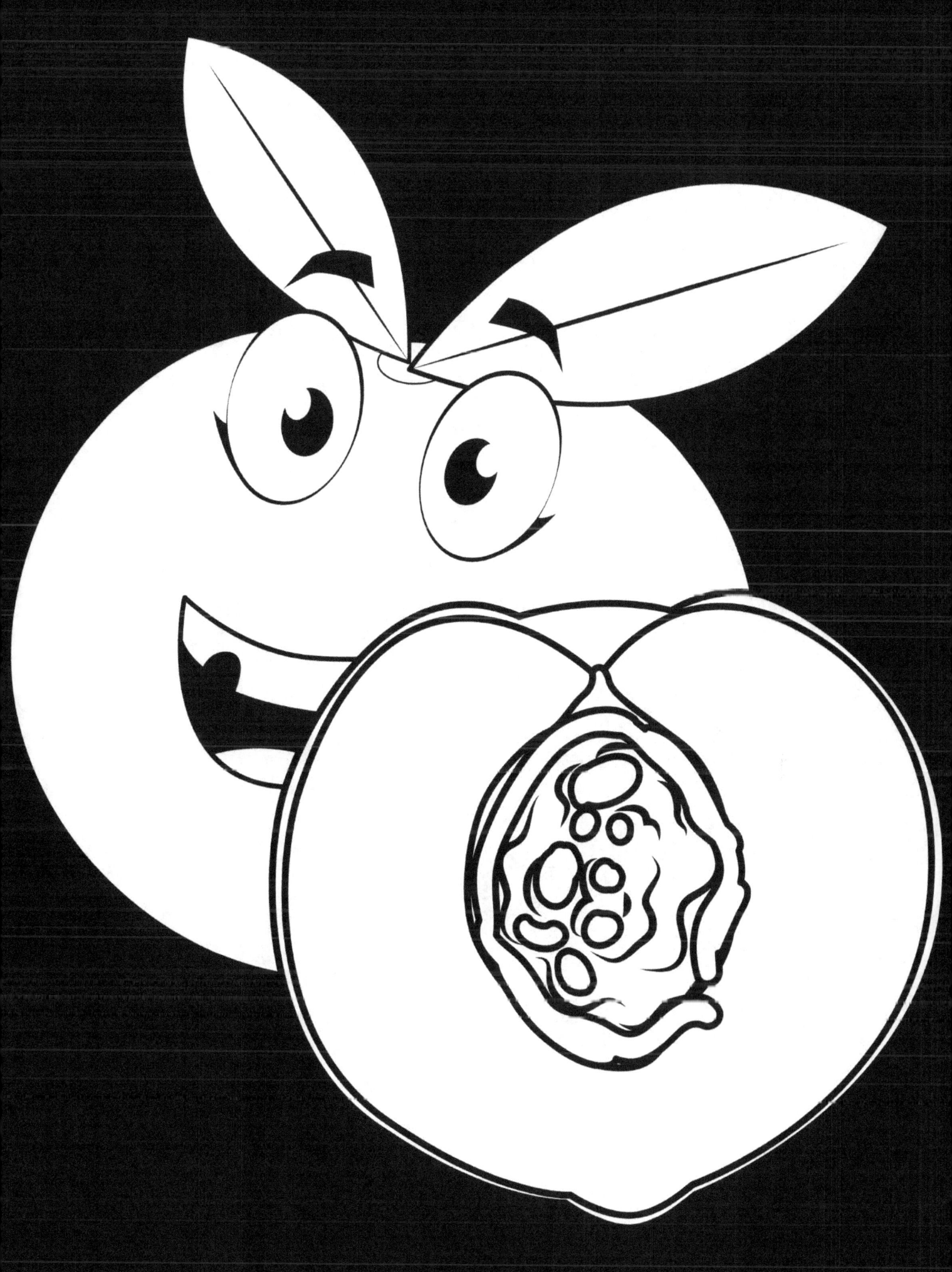

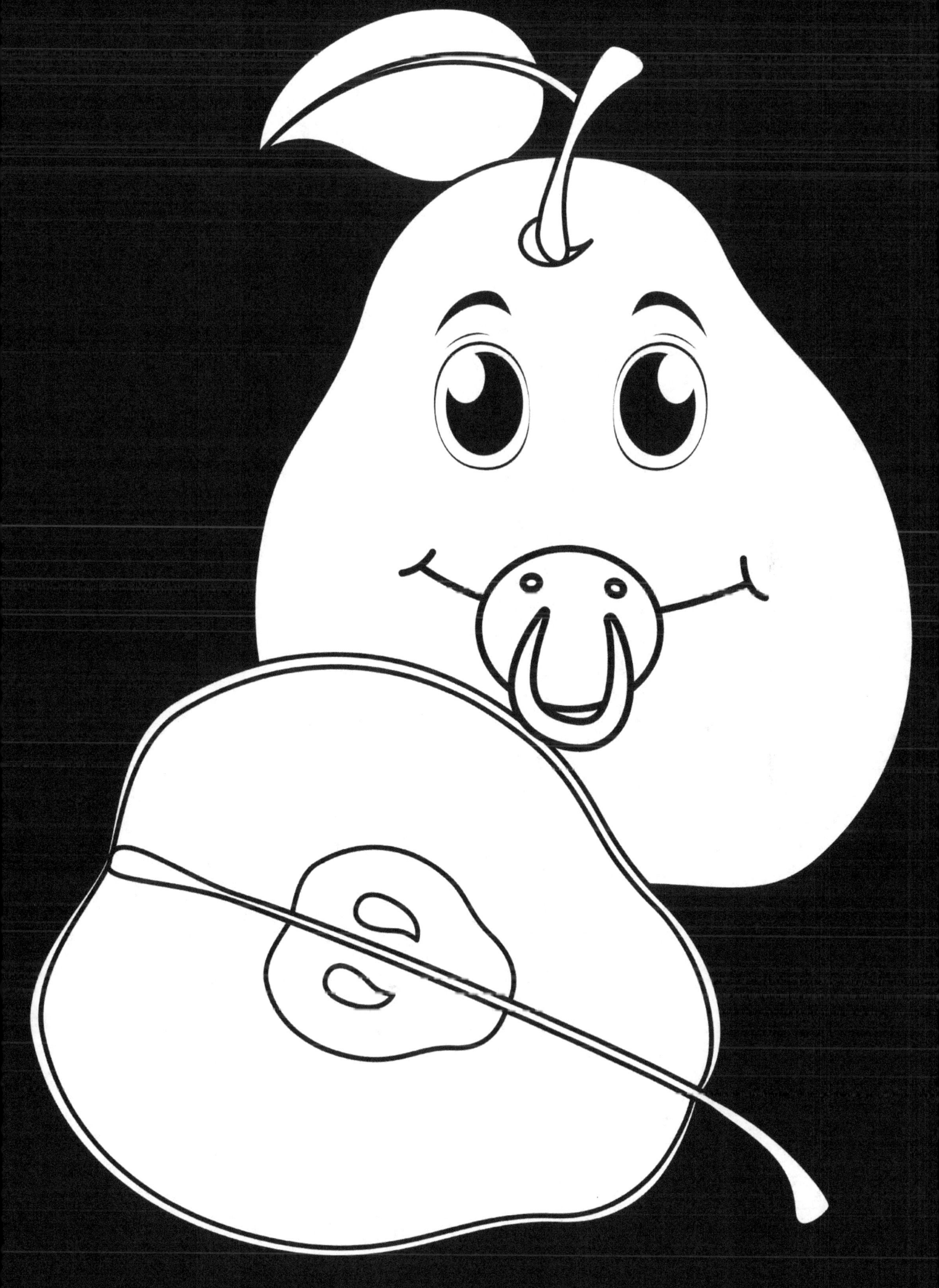

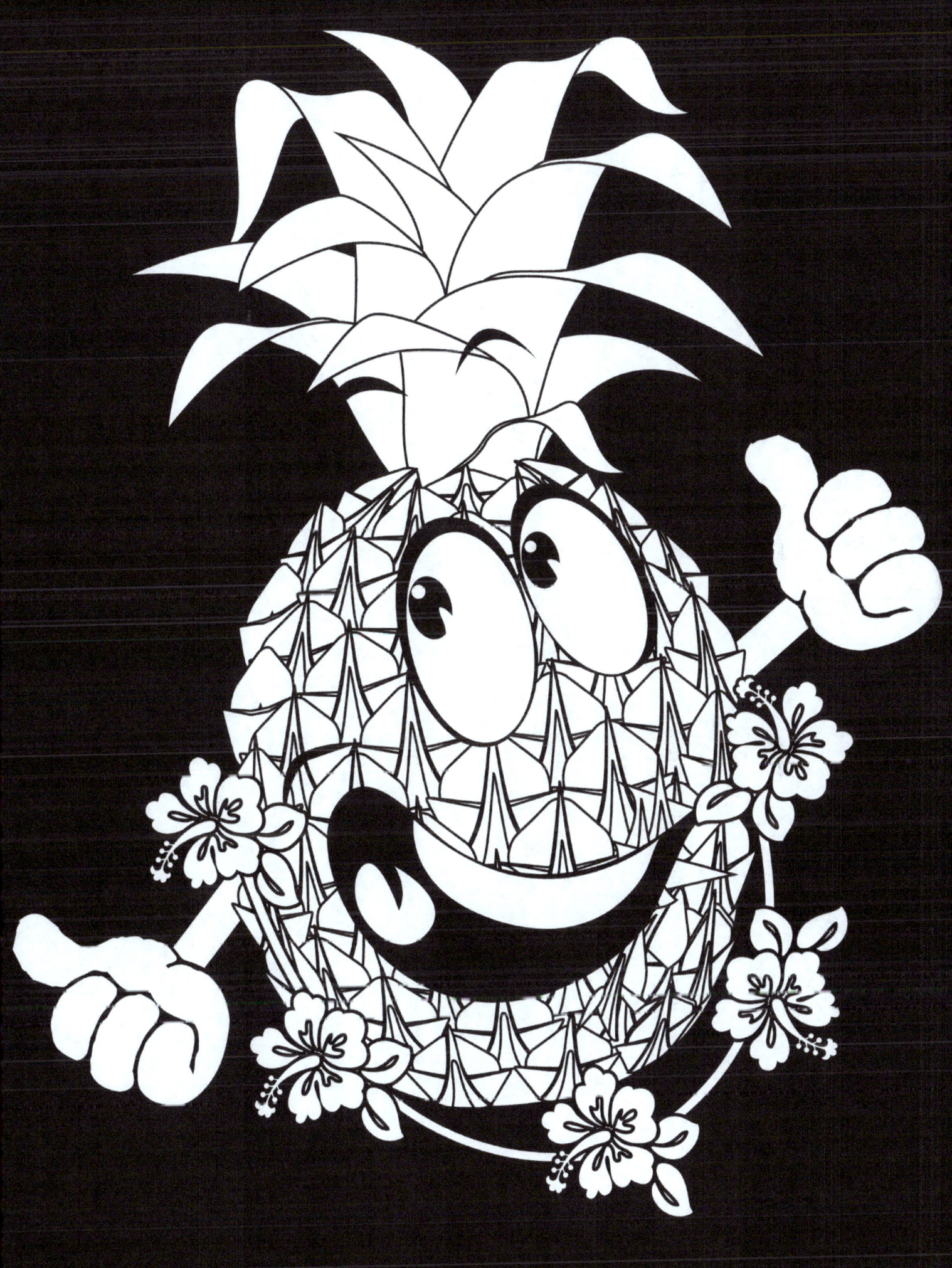

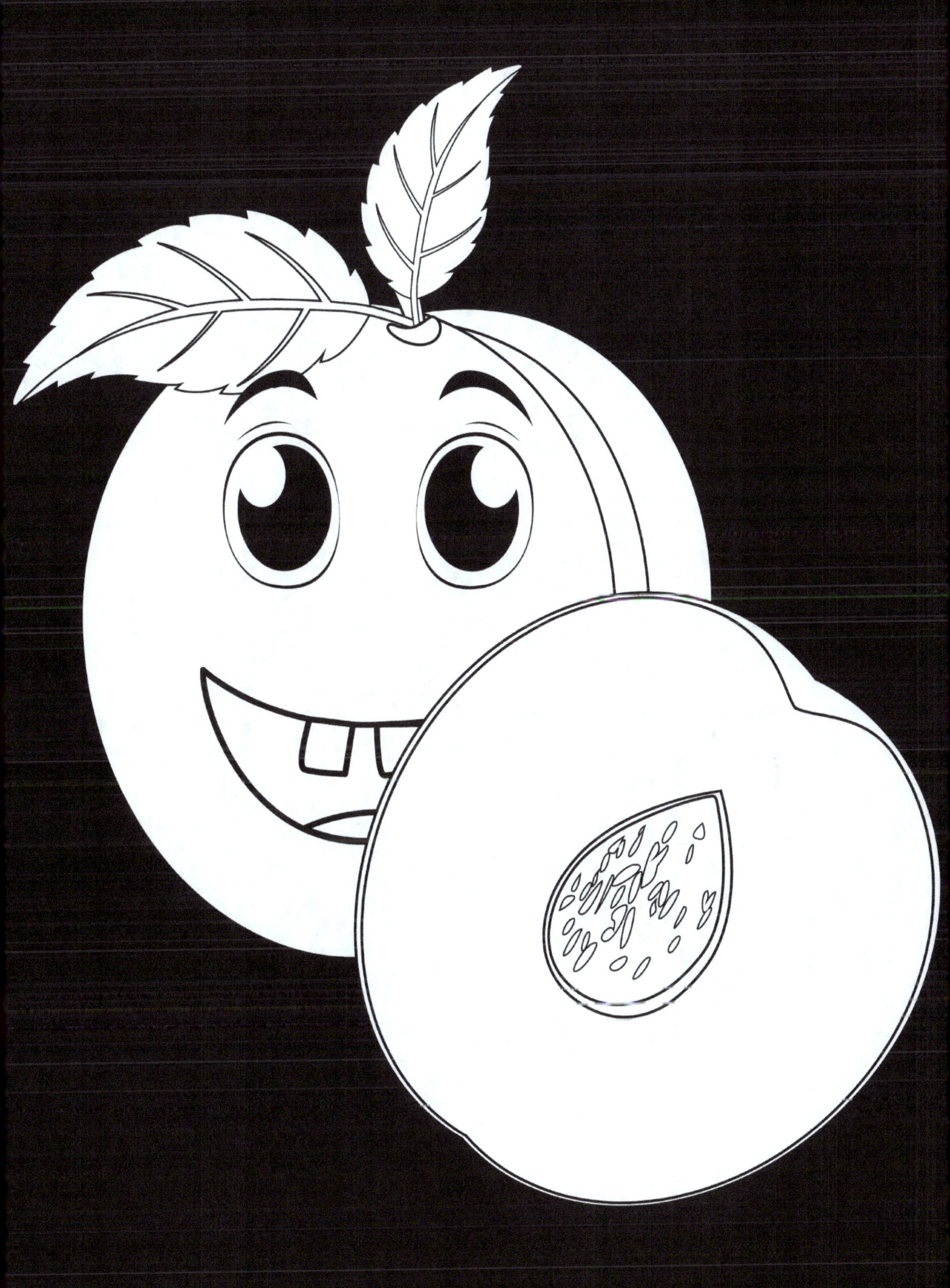

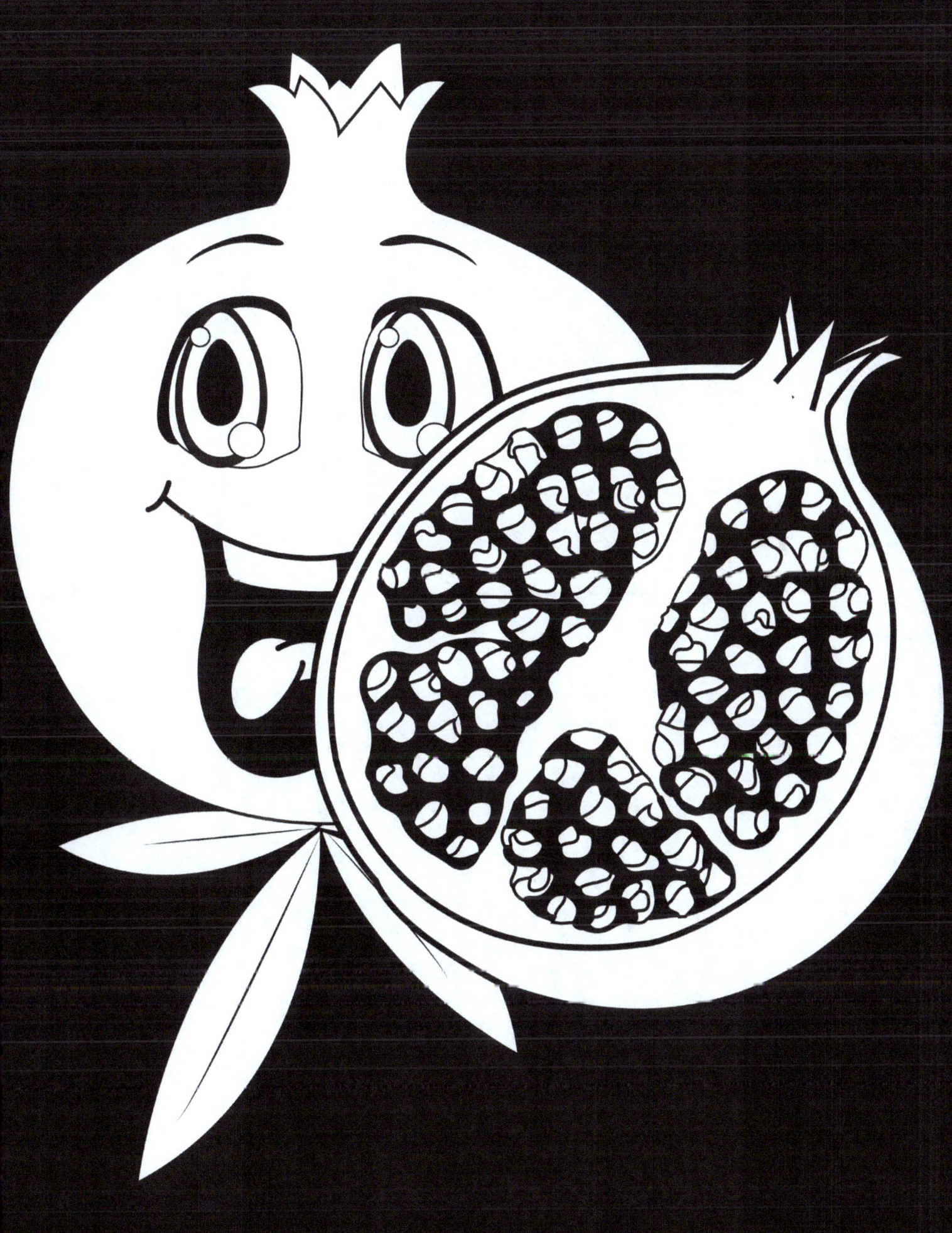

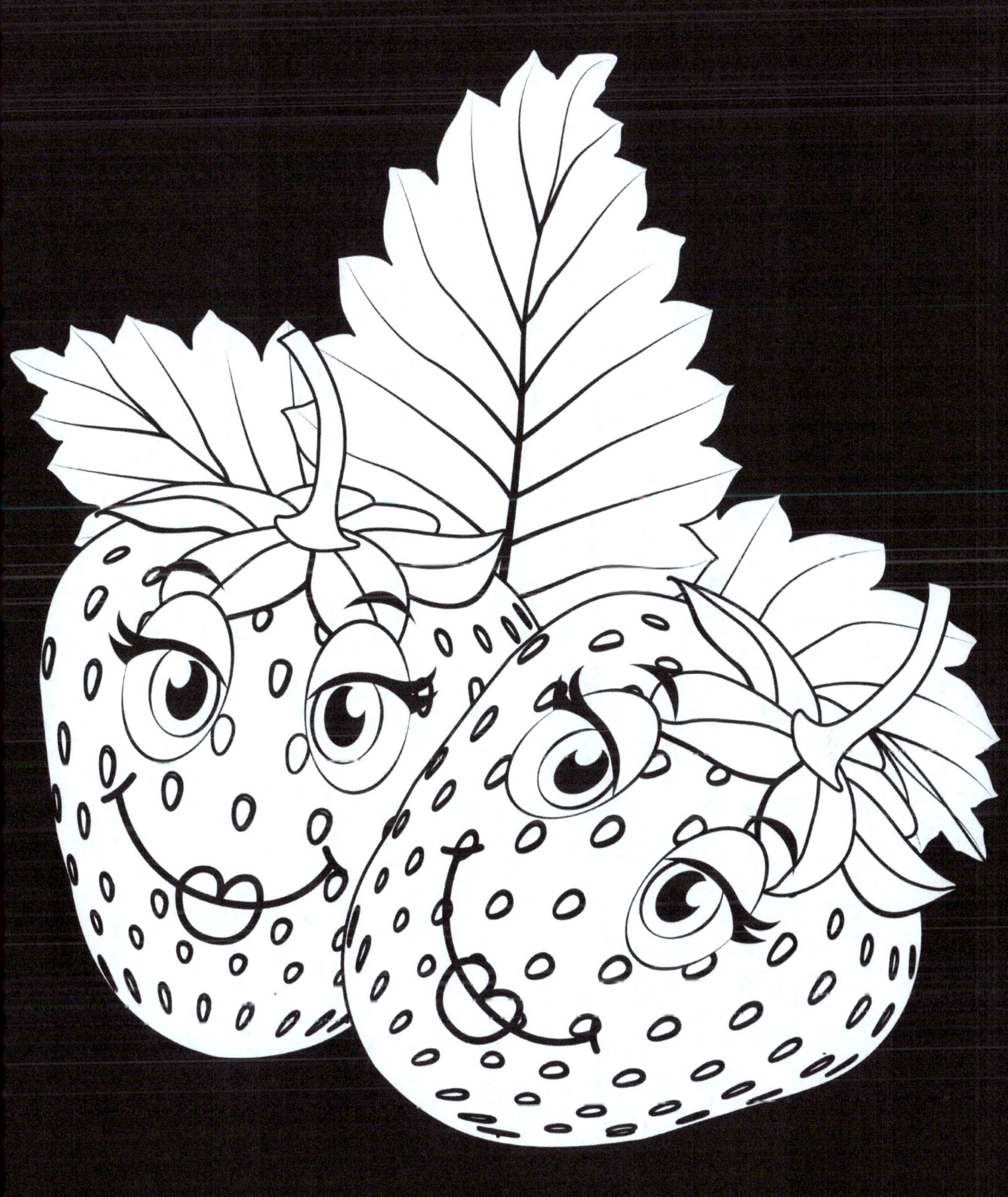

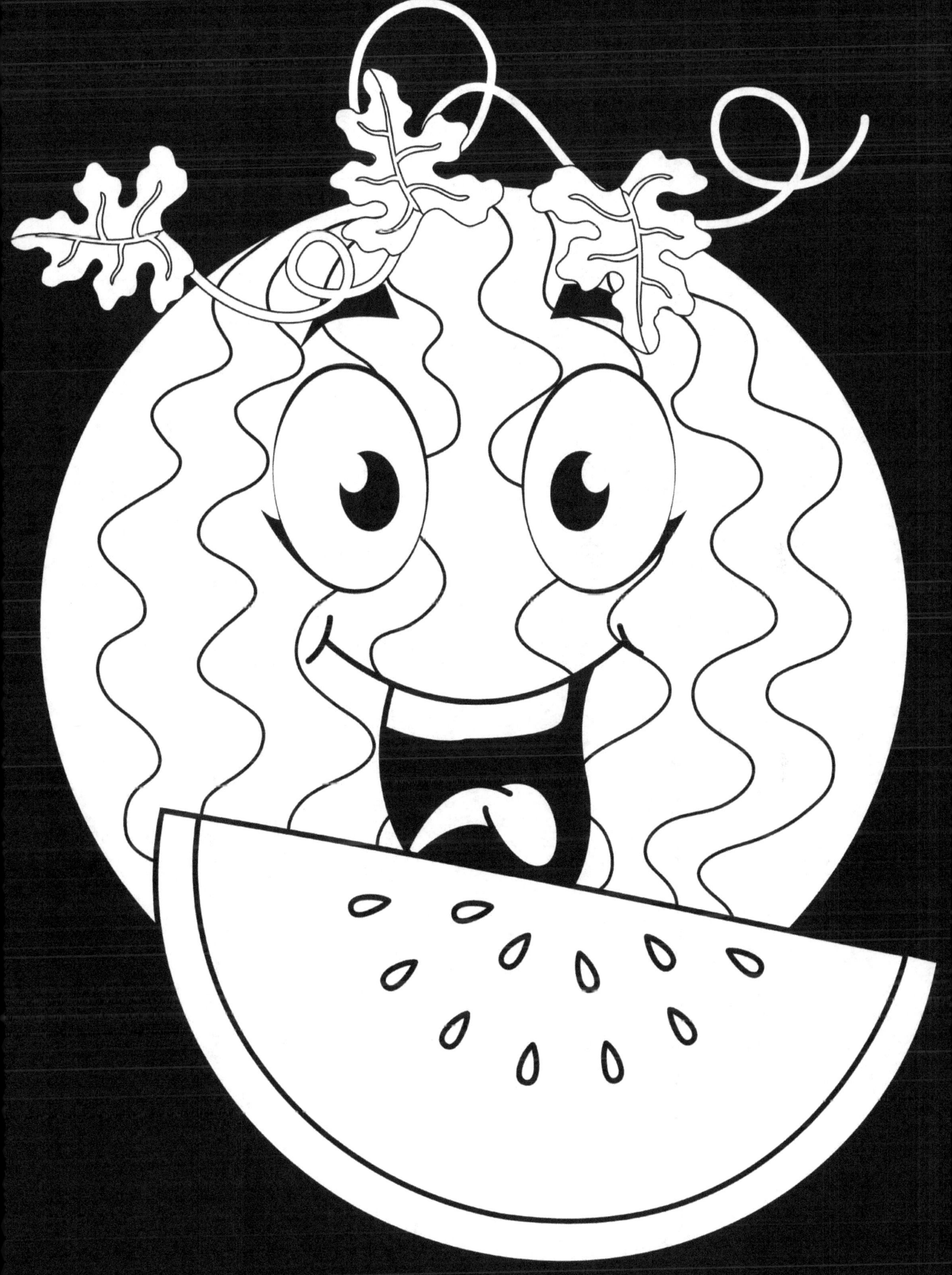

Thanks mom
for
this book
☺ I Love you!

Other Books by Author:

Lulu's Green Luge

Count with Kenny: 1-20

Selfish Little Bob, Selfish No More!

Pearl of the Indian Ocean

I Love Grandma

Where Are Ayden's Easter Eggs?

Christmas with Grandpa

Just Little Old Me

Thanks Lil Ren

Button

Button Goes to the Doctor

Button Goes to Hollywood

Button Finds Family and Friends at the Farm

Green Umbrella Coloring Book: Volume 2: ALPHABET (black Background)

www.ingramcontent.com/pod-product-compliance
Lightning Source LLC
Chambersburg PA
CBHW080713190526

45169CB00006B/2352